Joshua 1:9 This is my command — be strong and courageous! Do not be afraid or discouraged. For the Lord your God is with you wherever you go.

Every two minutes a child is diagnosed with cancer. My daughter became one of them when she was diagnosed with Ewing's sarcoma in her chest wall at three-months-old. I never would have believed childhood cancer could be the lowest funded form of cancer research. But like being shaken awake, my sweet little girl's reality of a life changed in the blink of an eye. Each day we are given, regardless the journey, the beginning or the ending, is a gift. It's up to us what we make of it. Beyond fear lies our freedom.
This is our beginning to getting there.
Through the glass.

Trisha Anderson
(Lilly Bumpus' mother)

© 2017 Kraken Books
Text © Trisha Anderson
Illustrations © Briana Ladwig

Published and produced by
Kraken Books Ltd.
1019 Skyview Drive
El Dorado, KS 67042

For more information on this book,
please check out
www.krakenbooks.com

ISBN: 978-0-9969742-0-2

Printed in the
United States of America
10 9 8 7 6 5 4 3 2 1

KRAKEN
BOOKS
Ltd.

Every two minutes a child is diagnosed with cancer. This book is dedicated to each of those children, some of whom will never see their childhood turn into adulthood. To my best friends Dalilah and Bailey—I will forever march on for you!

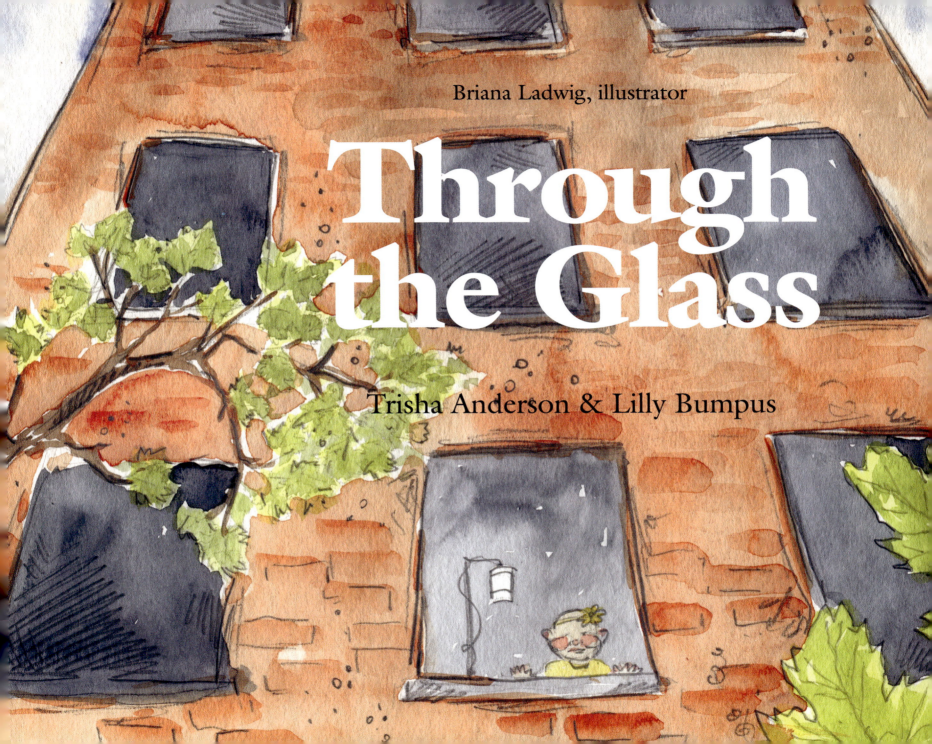

Briana Ladwig, illustrator

Through the Glass

Trisha Anderson & Lilly Bumpus

My mommy told me I was born
as the sun rose from deep within the earth.

She said my cheeks were as pink as the horizon
that began the new day.

I had ten tiny fingers and ten chubby toes.

She told me I had her red hair and when she
whispered in my ear,

"Mommy will never leave your side,"

I believed her.

Scans

I was too little to know my body was intended to work without struggle.

I was too little to know something called cancer came with me into this beautiful, yet dark world.

I was too little to know it had already chosen me.

I was too little to know why my mommy had to take me from doctor to doctor to lay in dark machine after dark machine.

Diagnosis

When moments got scary, Mommy would make the world disappear beyond the two of us.

When moments got loud, she hushed it out with a tender song only she and I could hear.

When Mommy heard I had cancer and I didn't yet know what it meant, I found all I needed within her soft smile.

Her pain matched mine as if she could feel the needles with each stick.

I found home inside my mommy. Inside love.

I was too little to know why Mommy would whisper in my tiny ears and promise me the world.

I was too little to know I had to fight to see it.

I was too little.

Round 1

As I rose to watch the sunrise glimmer diamonds
     and circles through the glass wall that
Mommy now called our home,

I noticed she slept in her shoes.

"It's Thanksgiving, sweet girl!" said Mommy, louder
than grown-ups usually do. Although her eyes looked
worn, I could see her smile within them.

"Today we will be thankful for whatever
we are given," she said as she put a new red hat
on my head.

Thanksgiving didn't bring the smell of food or the sound of family.

It brought chemotherapy.

When I was scared, Mommy would hold me tighter, and as if she took some pain away, I was revived.

Grown-ups called *doctors* and *nurses* liked to look at me a lot, but Mommy trusted them so I did, too.

Mommy told me to trust her when she whispered about a time she would call *"one day"* where nothing was as fresh as the blue sky. Where my feet touched the ground and the sun reached my face again.

Round 2

Days came and went.

Some days I only wanted to sleep so I could dream.

Some days I simply wanted to *live* instead of just being alive.

But all days came with chemotherapy

I was too little to know pain
was intended to diminish your smile.

So I smiled anyway.

Dreamed anyway.

Round 3

Some days I woke up before Mommy.

Before I opened my eyes I'd feel her warm arm draped over me and I knew.

It was her.

Some days I noticed her tangled in my wires and unaware.

I heard the nurses come in to check on me.
I closed my eyes and pretended to be asleep.

I waited to hear the door squeak shut
and the *sound* to fill the room.

The sound of silence.

Within the glass, within the wires,
I would watch my protector sleep.

Round 4

Chemotherapy took my red hair one strand at a time.

But I learned I didn't need it.

Mommy told me beauty grew inside me from the beautiful marks I left on the world.

That my beauty depended on my actions.

She told me I did this just by smiling.

Chemotherapy took my eyelashes one lash at a time, but I learned those, too, weren't needed.

My eyes could still see the world clearly without them.

Round 5

My favorite days were when Mommy would place me by the window where the busy world was below me.

They were too busy to look up at the glass where light knew no end, past the tall buildings as far as my eyes could see.

The sound of the street couldn't reach me.

I imagined the cars sounding like *my* beeping machines.

As the lights changed from red to green my world changed from one chemo to the next.

As people fought on the street I wondered if they fought cancer like I did?

Round 6

Some days I carried around a bucket in case my stomach hurt.

Sometimes I had to carry a bucket instead of toys.

Sometimes I wanted my toys and not to be sick.

One day I learned to carry both.

Some days I didn't want to push my pole, so I learned how to ride it.

Some days I didn't know how to be strong, but I learned I was stronger than I knew.

Resection

One early morning I lay in Mommy's arms as we were wheeled into a white room.

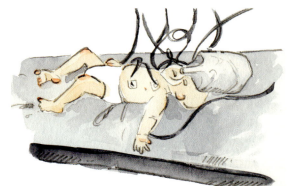

It was cold.

Mommy was cold.

"It's okay, Baby. Mommy is here," she whispered.

I naturally relaxed at her warm voice in my ear.

"Be strong, sweet girl. Mommy knows you are." And everything went dark before I could wonder what she meant.

When I woke up I knew I wasn't asleep for dreams.

A tube was coming out of my tummy, and when I squeezed my eyes closed I felt Mommy's hand fill mine and knew all would be okay.

Round 7

I would often hear giggles fill the halls and wonder where they were coming from.

I wouldn't have to wonder long before Mommy would open the door for me to see.

"Look, Baby!" she said as the breeze from the door opening hit my face like a hint of summer.

Our laughter would fill the halls.

Our dance moves would make more doors open.

They had *poles* just like me.
And *bald heads* just like me.

The doors always opened.

The rooms were always filled.

Round 8

"*Lillyyyyyy…."*

Sometimes my name would rain within the halls.

The innocent laugher in the air would call me out.

Mommy would swing the door open to discover an empty hallway.

She would tell me I had friends called angels.

I didn't know how they would walk all through life with me.

That no glass could keep them out.

That some—too many—had fallen before me.

And after me.

But I learned light always fights a way in. I'm many different forms of it.

Even in the form of an army of angels the eye cannot see.

Round 9

Chemotherapy kept coming.

Cancer kept coming.

My mommy's *silly faces* kept coming.

The sun still rose and fell.

And like magic, as the day changed to night
I secretly whispered,

"I'm coming for you, world. I'm coming home."

And I would dream of waves washing me home.

Round 10

Some days the hospital was so full they let us have sleep overs.

They would hang sheets from the ceiling and pretend they were walls.

I would watch the mommy next to us wear the same socks as *my* Mommy.

I would wait to sneak and peek over.

I'll be their friend, I told myself.

Sometimes I would share my toys.

Sometimes Mommy would share her dinner.

We always shared our love. Mommy said it was our family. And that's how you take care of family.

Round 11

"Your smile tells the world how deep your soul is," Mommy told me.

She said one picture could tell people what you felt without words.

I wondered what my smile said.

She told me something called *hope* existed through my smile.

So I smiled to every person I thought needed that thing Mommy called hope.

I thought my smile and happiness could change more than the darkness could.

Round 12

During my walks, I learned love comes from all different places.

Some places you have seen and some you have not.

Some love you can see and some you can only feel.

A love that knows no distance or bounds.

My mommy covered the walls in cards from people all over the world who loved me.

Each one with their own story.

Just like me.

Round 13

My mommy tried so hard to make me walk.
I was sure I wasn't ready. She held my hands and led me forward.
And as if bricks were in my slippers, I wouldn't budge. The doors would quickly open. My friends would sit at the doorway and try to get me to walk to them.
We giggled and whispered past bedtime as if we were sisters and brothers in a big house. That was home. They are forever my brothers and sisters.

Round 14

My "one day" is here.

My *last* chemotherapy.

My last NEED for medicine.

The start to the end is upon us.

A new beginning is before us.

My mommy tells me I'm cancer free!

Free from fighting a war called cancer.

Through the glass.
The light knows no bounds from here.
It curves and shapes within its limits.
I can reach out and touch it as if it were
waiting for me.
It makes my new red curls look like heaven
itself put tiny sprigs in them.
My mommy whispers in my ear each night as the
light falls to darkness, "Mommy will never leave
your side."

And I believe her.